A Life Course of
Miracles & Prayer

Supernatural Events in Ordinary Lives

PUBLISHED BY
OUR WRITTEN LIVES OF HOPE, LLC

Our Written Lives of Hope provides publishing services to authors in various educational, religious, and human service organizations. For information, visit www.owlofhope.com.

All rights reserved. No part of this publication may be reproduced, stored in a retrieval system, or transmitted in any form or by any means, without the permission of the copyright holders.

Copyright ©2014, Cathy Rodgers
Cover Photo by Cathy Rodgers
Proofing by Perrin Conrad, Conrad Copywriting
Cover & Layout Design by Rachael Hartman

Library of Congress Cataloging-in-Publication Data
Rodgers, Cathy 1958—
A Life Course of Miracles and Prayer:
Supernatural Events in Ordinary Lives (2nd Edition)

Library of Congress Control Number: 2015901238
ISBN: 978-1-942923-90-9

Unless specified otherwise, scripture quotations are taken from the New King James Version. Copyright ©1982 by Thomas Nelson, Inc. Used by permission. All rights reserved. Scripture quotations marked "KJV" are taken from the King James Version of the Bible.

A Life Course of *Miracles & Prayer*

Supernatural Events in Ordinary Lives

CATHY RODGERS

Contents

Dedication _____ 7

Introduction _____ 9

Chapter 1: The Family Threads of Prayer _____ 13

Chapter 2: Healings and Physicians _____ 19

Chapter 3: The Unknown _____ 29

Chapter 4: Mystical Visions _____ 37

Epilogue _____ 43

Dedication

This book is dedicated to my spiritual mentor and my Aunt, Dolores Smith. To my Mom, who always thought I could do anything. To my husband Bill, who supports all my endeavors, and to each of our children: Andi, Jeff, Jon and Candice. To our grandsons William and Charley, you are now on high alert to be on the lookout for miracles!

Most of all, this is for the next generation, so they will know that God was, is, and always will be in the miracle business.

In Loving Memory of:

Wade and Cora Conder
Helen Elizabeth Conder
Cody Holloway
Morgan Kathleen Green

Introduction

Miracles and unexplained phenomena seem to be discounted for what they are through rationalization or by trying to over explain extraordinary events. These intersections with potential disaster are sometimes shoved to the background with a label, "Oh, that was good luck," or "That happened a long time ago."

Maybe that's why miracles were not discussed at my childhood dinner table, or it could have been a way to avoid calling others in the family "crazy" or "extreme."

My Aunt Dolores was known as the extremist in our family. When cousins gathered and her name came up, the term "religious fanatic" was used a lot. I was never sure why the term applied, except she thought differently about the world, as I knew it, and went to church a lot.

Throughout the years, my aunt talked to me about little stories that could only be explained as miracles from God. I was able to convince her to record her thoughts so that others could learn about the amazing things that have happened during her life.

Dolores Smith lives in Cocoa, Florida, and is a woman known for keeping the prayer line to heaven "hot." The Bible has served as the blueprint for her life and she continues to study and learn from scripture. Now in her mid-80's, she is a prayer warrior for her entire family, network of friends, and even our nation.

She experiences good health, has a Christian message recording ministry and has managed to reproduce over 2,000 cassette tapes, 3,000 CDs, and many videos right in her own home. She does this for family, friends and her intercessory prayer group, "The Jesus Believers."

Dolores retired as a bookkeeper and business owner of a family-owned furniture store. She currently has two children who have given her five grandchildren and four great-grandchildren. She is a humble, yet outspoken woman and could even be considered an ordinary person. However, these miraculous events have made her life truly extraordinary. In fact, there have been many more miracles which have taken place that are not recorded here because she has found they are difficult to separate from her everyday life.

I was told these accounts of miracles over the course of several years, orally and through writings and recordings. The final proof even went back and forth by e-mail, since she purchased a computer at the age of 79. Her mini notepad paper with handwritten notes in print (never cursive) has always been something to treasure. She is very methodical about cataloging recordings, DVDs and Bible verses for various subjects and has always been willing to share her resources with those around her. I certainly wish I had the generous gift of memory that she has; her mind is extremely sharp when it comes to recalling events.

Because I have only known her to be truthful (and extremely careful about being so), I believe each and every account and have no reason to believe otherwise.

She has never altered her mind with alcohol or medications.

The fact that God allows ordinary people to see phenomenal miracles is something that should be shared, not only in our families, but also with everyone we encounter.

I've considered that miracles don't just happen without a lot of prayer. Certainly emergency answers to prayer do happen. Perhaps the unexplained healings, breakthroughs and unusual, time altering things that occur beyond human understanding and reasoning are not linked to the prayer of the moment, but to the prayers of a lifetime.

For the eyes of the Lord are on the righteous, And His ears are open to their prayers. - 1 Peter 3:12a NKJV.

Dolores Smith with one of her great-granddaughters.

Chapter 1

THE FAMILY THREADS OF PRAYER

Discovering the secrets of my family tree was something I had never pursued, until recently. For years, I heard family members talk about how we may be descendants of Cherokee Indians. I had romantic notions of meeting my ancestors, calculated my percentage of heritage, and just knew that's where my brown eyes had come from. I held on to that hope even to the end, but found out after my grandmother's death that it just wasn't true. I had to wait a long time, because she lived to be 101 years old.

A few years earlier, my husband began tracing his roots back to Charleston, South Carolina. It was exciting to visit the Confederate Home on Broad Street where his great grandmother used to live, and discover that she had a window at a local church dedicated to her. We had heard about the old family mansion, but to see the house in person, complete with Tiffany windows, now transformed into a glorious Bed & Breakfast, was amazing.

After those dreamy trips to South Carolina, I was afraid to dig too deep into my own background for fear of finding horse thieves or carpetbaggers, but later I began putting together all the stories my aunt told me.

Fighting off the Angel of Death

My Aunt Dolores grew up in Charlotte with two brothers who both came close to death. She recalled her two-year-old baby brother crying when his legs hurt. It can best be described as the feeling one has when a limb falls asleep. He had simultaneous numbness and prickly pain. The doctors didn't know what was wrong, but offered to cast both legs. Since there was no diagnosis, this treatment was refused.

Night after night she watched her mother hum and massage those aching legs while they all listened to the radio. The doctors said her brother could never walk again. Years later, after an epidemic hit America, they realized he had been struck with polio. By this time, hospital wings were filled with people in iron lungs, many were in wheelchairs, and some never walked again.

Well, that little boy was my father, and he not only overcame polio, but he also learned to walk all over again. My aunt recalls vividly the day she was in the living room on her tricycle when my grandfather called out for my dad to walk to him.

Now, my grandmother was not the most warm and fuzzy person, nor did she ever speak of her faith. It was a "wow" moment when I learned of this miracle of survival happening because I know in my heart she prayed.

Soon, my Uncle Jerry came down with diphtheria,

known as the "the strangling angel of children," and he required around-the-clock care. The family doctor spent the first two nights with him until a neighbor, who was a retired nurse, volunteered to come and help so that my grandmother could rest. Jerry was given alcohol baths to reduce the high fevers, and his throat was swabbed every thirty minutes with medicine. He was so contagious the doctor would not admit him to the hospital. He remained only semi-conscious for about four or five days due to the raging fever.

My father got a mild case of the disease since the boys shared a bedroom. Then everyone else in the house was inoculated, including Aunt Dolores. She recalls being chased down with a "foot long needle" and two people holding her down to give her a shot.

Word was sent to a relative to come and help with the cooking and laundry. All the linens had to be changed every 24 hours and disinfected in a huge pot of boiling water before they were hand washed. All the dishes were also put into boiling water before being washed. My aunt recalls staying home from school for about three weeks with big yellow danger signs around the house and playing with no friends or neighbors for what seemed like an eternity.

My grandfather was also a man of prayer. He learned to rely on faith and prayer during all that sickness under his roof, while working low-level jobs to provide for his family during the depression. He worked at a furniture store as a salesman, drove a laundry truck (before washing machines) and drove a coal truck.

Apparently he was very particular about being clean, and he disliked those dirty jobs so much that he would throw up the minute he got home. But he never quit.

Rumors of deaths in the city were rampant, and unfortunately, many were true. But there was miraculous survival in this house. It was an answer to prayers from not only my grandparents, but also a doctor, neighbors and family members.

Family Saved from Crash

On a dark summer morning, Dolores Smith departed Charlotte, North Carolina. She was heading back to Orlando with her mother, father and son. Her brother Jerry had just picked a whole box of fresh tomatoes grown in his garden to send back with them, and they were parked safely in the back seat between her mother and father (my grandparents).

There was very little traffic on the interstate that morning, but suddenly, a big semi-truck passed their car and then slowed down. Then it passed them again and slowed down. A third time the truck passed and slowed down, but this time the back end slightly touched the rear bumper of their car. "It happened so fast; I did not even have a chance to apply my brakes, even though I can remember my foot got on the brakes," she recalled.

The impact of the large semi-truck threw their car into a swerve. It was very quick. The car went back and forth on the highway and slammed down the beginning of an embankment.

Suddenly the front end of their car was suspended, and "it was like giant hands pushed on my car. It felt like a balloon inflating below. Yes, it's the only thing I can think of to describe it, like a balloon just going swoosh, swoosh, swoosh," recalled Dolores.

The "balloon cushion" stopped the car a little bit at a time and the car rolled gently between two metal posts. It stopped right at the edge of the hill.

"I sat there for a second in shock, and when I looked around, we had not even lost one tomato out of that box. Mom and Dad were sitting there, and I think it was either Father or Mother, I am not sure which, said 'I sure believe in angels now!'

"My son, John, had been travelling in the front seat with a pillow. He ended up on the floorboard with that pillow over his head. As if time stood still for a few moments, I had a delayed reaction of shock. Suddenly, I knew there was absolutely no question that angels had stopped that car!"

Three praying souls and not one tomato moved!

Without a Scratch

At the age of about 80, my grandfather was riding his big three-wheeled bicycle in his neighborhood. He loved to get out in the fresh air and see what was happening. On this day, he was not paying very much attention, when a pickup truck full of equipment backed out of a driveway, hit him and threw him into a ditch.

The man in the truck heard a noise and immediately

stopped, only to find the big metal three-wheeled bicycle completely wrapped around my grandfather. The bicycle was so twisted around his body that there was no way the man could get him out. But he kept trying and was finally able to free him from the mangled wire. Instead of crying out in pain or begging for an ambulance, the only thing my grandfather wanted to do was get home to take a shower and get all the dirt off of him.

My aunt recalled that the man in the truck was terribly upset. He wanted to take Grandpa to the emergency room, but Grandpa refused. He was not hurt in any way, and did not have a visible scratch or a bruise on him! The man was really insistent to get Grandpa to the emergency room. After all, how is it possible to get hit by a truck, have a bicycle wrapped around you, and not have internal damages?

The truck driver called about two hours later and again the next morning to check on Grandpa, but he was just fine. The driver decided the least he could do was to buy him a brand new three-wheel bicycle, so he happily made the delivery a few days later.

Chapter 2

HEALINGS AND PHYSICIANS

Right in Front of My Eyes

And He said to her, "Daughter, your faith has made you well. Go in peace, and be healed of your affliction."
Mark 5:34

While pulling a door closed behind her, Dolores Smith caught her finger on the latch. When the door slammed, it totally crushed her finger and cut her extremely badly. It was so severe that one side of the fingernail was crushed, and on the other side, the flesh was just pulverized. "I could see the bone and the little tendons sticking out and almost fainted right then. I got very ill and recall collapsing into a chair right inside," she said.

"I just held my finger up and I said, 'Jesus,' and instantly the finger began to heal in front of my eyes. It was really strange because even though it happened very, very fast, I watched my finger heal in layers. I saw the process work just like a small knitting machine. The flesh kept joining together back and forth, back and forth like a little weaving loom, and then the tendons suddenly reattached. The whole thing probably took only 30 seconds, but I was allowed to see this in slow motion."

Dolores remembers looking at her finger in complete amazement and saying, "I don't believe it!"

"Well, I learned a lesson right then which I remember to this day. I learned that what you say is really important, because when I said, 'I don't believe it,' which was only an expression, once the word 'don't' came out of my mouth, the healing stopped that second, just like when you slam on the brakes."

"The good news is the finger was completely healed in that top layer of flesh. It was slightly red to look at, like a wound that was recovering. I feel if I had not said the word 'don't,' I would have seen white skin, but nevertheless it was not sore, it did not hurt, and there was NO pain. I had a typewriter on my desk at that time, and I ran over and began to type something using that finger and it was totally normal in every way. So I feel that was a really big miracle that God performed."

Instant Healing from Gallstone Pain

Dolores woke up one morning in extreme pain. My uncle offered to take her straight to the emergency room, but she insisted he go ahead and perk the morning coffee, even though it was 4:00 a.m. While he was in the kitchen, she began to pray.

"The pain was so unbearable I could not get out

of the bed. We suspect it was a gallstone. But, while I was praying, the Lord brought to my mind the name James Black. James and his wife were friends of ours. I felt commanded by the Lord to call him, but was a little surprised because his wife prayed for people, but James never did that. He was a very quiet person, a background type of person, yet a devout Christian. The thought would not leave, and I knew he was the one I was to call.

"So I waited, while groaning in extreme pain, until about 7:30 or 8:00, somewhere along in there, and I called their house. James answered the phone and said, 'I'll get Nancy.' I still recall my response. I said, 'No, I don't want Nancy, I want you James. The Lord told me to have you come pray for me.' He said, 'Well, I'll see if I can get Nancy.' I said, 'No, it is to be you, James. You have to come.'" Even though he was on the spot, James agreed.

James and Nancy arrived about 30 minutes later. "When they came to the bedroom door, Nancy came forward, but I put my hand up and said, 'No, Nancy, James is supposed to pray for me.'

"So James came to the end of my bed and he just put his hand where my feet were under the covers. The very second (he hardly had a chance to pray, but did say a few short words) he touched my foot, and a warm healing began at my feet and went straight on up to my head. I could feel a sensation go through my body. I had instant healing, and I mean instant! At that moment, I jumped out of the bed and said, 'Would y'all like some coffee?'" James and Nancy were too surprised to answer. "They had only been in the house about a minute, yet that is how quick the healing took place! I just praise God for that."

A Wasted Trip to the Emergency Room?

When my cousin, John Smith, was about six years old, he fell off of his bicycle and split his knee open. The wound exposed the bone. Dolores washed off the knee, wrapped it in a wet towel, and rushed her son to the emergency room.

She recalls, "Before going into the emergency room, John and I prayed together in the car for him to be healed." The injury was extreme, and something needed to be done immediately. They went inside and answered questions while a nurse washed the raw bloody knee, then gave him a small towel to hold in his hands to blot the blood. The nurse told them John was the next patient in line.

"So while sitting there and wondering about the outcome, I recall just staring at his uncovered knee. When all of a sudden, it mended in front of my eyes! John did not even know it. I mean, it happened with just a zwoopp! That knee was completely made whole and healed, except for a little redness where it had been scraped.

Dolores' mouth hung open. She and John looked at each other, neither saying a word.

"I opened my mouth to say something, but just at

that second, the nurse came out and said, 'Next.' John jumped up and followed her to the exam room. I was still sitting in the chair, but quickly got up and followed them. When I walked in, the doctor looked at me like I was crazy! I guess he had seen distraught mothers before, but he looked at me and said, 'Well, let's just put a big Band-Aid on this.' He acted like I was really juvenile."

"Looking back, we were both shocked, but why are we shocked when God does what we pray for?!"

The "big Band-Aid" was administered with a shaking head and a large bill. "So we left. I never did say anything, which I should have, but it was like the words would not come. Well, the nurse that cleaned up the knee knew it, and the lady doing the information desk stuff knew it. I don't know what they discussed later, but John's knee was 100% healed."

Another Wasted Trip to the Doctor?

When John, was about 10 years old, he had another accident on his bicycle. This time he got some of that really fine gravel from his crash on the paved road imbedded into the dirty, bloody palm of his hand.

There seemed to be no way around going to the doctor's office, so on the way for help, my Aunt Dolores prayed in the car. "Just when the nurse called us back to the exam room, I looked down at John's hand. It was still a mess. But, the minute we got inside the exam room and by the time the doctor held it up to take a look, new skin appeared on his hand!"

"I can still remember the look on the doctor's face when he said, 'Why are you here?' John answered, 'Well, it was bad when I came in here.'"

My aunt pondered, "I do not know why God does things in this order or why we are supposed to just wait and wait sometimes, but the hand was healed right before the doctor came in! The doctor, of course, thought we were both nuts again, but this was a different physician than a few years earlier." Dolores says it's just another example of God answering their prayers for healing.

Instant Relief from a Migraine

During the 80's, Dolores was traveling between Cocoa and Orlando on business one day, when a migraine suddenly came upon her. She had suffered with migraines for 30 years, so she knew what would happen if she didn't take action to stop it. "If I did not find a quiet place to be alone quickly, I would be totally out of commission within minutes."

Because her senses were dulled, she had to drive carefully. "I recall driving slower than normal, but it was getting worse by the second. Finally, I realized I had to pull over. I did see a service station, but it looked like a really bad place to stop. I remember thinking, what am I going to do?

"All of a sudden, I believe the Lord put an old friend's name in my mind – someone I had not seen in maybe three or four years. It dawned on me; she only lived maybe a mile from where I was at that moment. I thought if I could just get to Louise Walter's house..."

"The headaches are normally blinding, but somehow I made it up to her house. By the time Louise came to the door, I was shaking and trembling really badly. She said, 'Well, hello Dolores,' and I said, 'Can I go to bed in your house?' as if this was a normal type of thing and she said, 'Of course, come right on in.'

"Well she herself was a person who has migraines. She could tell by looking at me that my color was really bad, and knew I was really sick. So she took me to a guest bedroom and said, 'I will be right back.'

"She brought me an ice pack. By this time, I barely knew she was in the room. But I do remember her putting her hand on my foot and praying. Well, as she began to pray, it was just like electricity began running through my body. It started at my feet and went up to my head. When it hit my head, all of a sudden the pain left, and I went into a deep sleep right that minute."

When Dolores woke up to food cooking in the kitchen about three hours later, she was totally refreshed from good sleep and back to normal.

"We both enjoyed a beautiful dinner together, and I know without a doubt I was healed that day," she said.

Defying All Odds

My grandparents lived in an apartment that was attached to my aunt and uncle's home. So on the day my grandfather, J. Wade Conder, experienced a heart attack, Aunt Dolores was close by.

My cousin Sandra called the hospital ahead of time, so while my aunt was driving Grandpa to the hospital, a team of doctors were busy preparing for his arrival.

Dolores recalls, "After the initial examination, the doctors said his heart was like soft jelly. Because he was so old, it had not exploded. But he had something like a gradual leak, and when that was completed, he would die. They gave him 20 minutes to live.

"I looked into his room, and he was sitting up chatting away, just having a good time talking to the doctors. He did not even look sick to me, but the doctors said he had a very limited time. So I called home to get the rest of the family there. But instead of dying in a short amount of time, he was moved up to ICU. He stayed in ICU about three weeks and then progressed to a regular room for two weeks.

"They kept telling me during that first week there was simply no way his heart could continue to work, because not only was it like a bunch of jelly, but it was not working properly at all.

"I was not prepared for him to go at that time. It was 1979. I just remember praying and praying that I was just simply not ready to lose my father at that time, but wanted him to live, and if God really didn't mind, to please let him live.

"And Dad lived. When we got ready to leave the hospital after five weeks, I asked the doctor what his physical or diet limitations may be. That's when I remember his physician throwing his hands up in the air saying, 'There is no way that this man can even be alive. Let him do whatever he wants to do! I have no clue.' But Dad lived 10 years beyond that time, even though they said there was no way his heart could make it."

J. Wade Conder lived from October 29, 1904 to December 5, 1989.

Chapter 3

THE UNKNOWN

Hope in Tragedy

When the 80-and-over members of the Jesus Believers came together in February 2014, each participant was asked to tell the group one of the most memorable ways God had made a difference in their lives. The story Dolores chose reflected the miracle back to God, while taking the light off her.

"Back in the 80's our family moved to Brevard County to open a second furniture store. Not long after the move, the flagship store in Orlando burned and everything was lost. Dealing with the insurance company and the fire department was still fresh on my mind when I went back to Orlando for a Women's Aglow meeting on a Saturday.

"While having lunch, I was talking to a lady who sat next to me. As we were getting to know one another, I told her we used to live in the area and that our business just burned. Even though we had opened a second store in Cocoa, that store had just not taken off yet and was not producing a lot of income. But when we lost the Orlando location, our business in Cocoa tripled. So we never experienced a loss; we had the same amount of money, and God did not let us go without income! I told her I had joy and peace about the whole thing."

"Well, I had forgotten about this encounter until five years later. It was a Saturday morning and I just happened to be working in our store catching up on some bookkeeping when a lady walked in the door asking for me. It was the same woman I met at the Aglow meeting years ago, and she told me she was in town on business, had remembered the name of our store, and just wanted to drop in to say thank you.

"I asked her what she wanted to thank me for, and even though I no longer remember her name, I will never forget her reply. She said, 'Before I met you, I was planning on committing suicide. There were just no answers and I couldn't see any hope. But I realized what happened to you was much worse than what I was going through and God was taking care of you. That's why I didn't commit suicide.'"

Dolores surmised that when God has used us in some way, most of the time we never know about it, but this time he let her know.

Praying for a Stranger

Back in the late 70's, Dolores Smith belonged to a prayer group that met on a regular basis. One day, they got a call that a young girl in their church named Lisa had been in a horrible automobile accident.

Lisa, who was getting married about three months from that time, had a broken leg, a crushed pelvis and a crushed bone fragment next to her spinal cord they could not reach. Doctors feared an operation may kill her, and she was facing permanent paralysis at the age of 21.

The prayer group agreed that members would rotate, going to the hospital every day to pray for Lisa and encourage her. "She was really excited because we would tell her that God could heal her and that she was to keep thinking positive and to believe. So she was doing this."

Lisa's family and the pastor of her church became very upset about the prayer group offering the hope of healing. Lisa's mother talked to the pastor, and they agreed with the doctors that there was absolutely no way that she would ever walk. They asked that the prayer group stop going to see her and offering "false hope."

"We did not go back to see her in the hospital because they stopped us, but we continued to pray and to believe." Even after Lisa got out of the hospital and during her rehabilitation, the group continued to believe and pray.

"Well, all of a sudden, her pelvis got healed and Lisa was able to start walking." The doctors were amazed, because this could not be replaced or fixed by man, yet the x-rays revealed her bones were restored."

Six months later, Lisa was able to walk down the aisle and was married by that very same preacher who did not believe in miracles. "The church members continued to deny that healing, even when it was right in front of their eyes."

A Supernatural Escape

This incident happened to Aunt Dolores long before she got married. "My two girlfriends and I decided we wanted to go somewhere for the 4th of July weekend, and we didn't want to go to the beach with everybody else, so we made reservations at a hotel in Asheville, North Carolina. We were all out of high school and working, so we rented a car to go sightseeing. My friend Edna, who was known to be very hot tempered, was the one driving on this particular day.

They were about five miles outside of Asheville on a three-lane highway, with the middle lane used for turning and passing. Edna was known to have a "heavy foot" and was living up to her reputation on this day. "Meanwhile, two boys trying to flirt with us passed us driving this hot rod. Edna was not in the mood for any of that, so when they passed us and slowed down, Edna sped up and passed them. Well, in just a few minutes, the same thing happened and they sped up and passed us.

"Edna was really angry by this time. But up ahead, it looked like a car was coming toward us in the middle lane and a second car was waiting for us to come through before they turned. This second car was waiting in the middle lane. But right at this exact moment, a vehicle came up beside them and the boys were equal to the car in the middle lane. So right at that moment, there were three cars in each one of the lanes, and there was almost no room left.

"Our hot-headed Edna went zooming about 90 miles an hour, and we went between the car that was waiting to turn and the boys in the hot rod car. We went right between them! Dot, the girl on my left, started screaming and I just started praying to myself silently. I thought about turning the ignition off but that would make us wreck too.

"Let me tell you, there was no room to go through, absolutely no room to go through those two vehicles. When we went between those cars, the angels must have done it, because it's the only possible explanation.

"Meanwhile, Edna kept zooming down the road and finally pulled over about a mile away. We all took a deep breath! I think there was a slight paint exchange on one side, which was not even a scratch to speak of. This was another miracle in driving, and God must have intervened because there was no way we could have gotten through without being killed or badly hurt. But we were seen through, yet another time. Praise the Lord!!"

When The Unexplained Interrupts Time

It was around the year 2008, at an intersection in Cocoa. Dolores was preparing to turn right, just as the car across from her began turning left, directly into her path. "I'm pretty sure I had the right of way," she says.

"The man and I eyeballed each other... there was NO WAY either one could stop in time, as we were extremely close to crashing into each other.

"Suddenly, the front end of my car was picked up and moved over close to the curb. That man had total shock on his face as he passed on by, because He also experienced this supernatural event.

"I pulled into a nearby parking lot and allowed my heart to get back to normal, which took about 3-5 minutes. Then I praised God for quite a long while for sparing my life! Every once in a while, when I remember the incident, I praise Him again."

Being Willing and Able

Dolores volunteered her time for over seven years at TV 52, a local Christian station in Cocoa. She helped with telethons, answered the phone and prayed with individuals who called in.

While being interviewed on the air in 1988 by Stephen Kiser, host of the "Believers Lifestyle" show, she said, "Before there was a TV station here, God spoke to me out loud in my automobile and said, You're going to be on Christian television and I began to laugh. At that time, I could not see how that could come to pass with no television station anywhere near."

While keeping this incident totally to herself, Dolores asked for forgiveness, because even though she was not a speaker or a TV personality, she knew that God could equip her to do anything – even if it was beyond her reach. Later on, she found out that 99% of people are not in front of the TV cameras, but working behind the scenes.

Within two years of hearing that message in her car, a station had come to town, so Dolores made herself available when they advertised for prayer partners. Her volunteer work included helping with whatever they needed at the station. That often meant answering the phone with someone in a desperate situation or circumstance on the other end.

To Dolores' amazement, she would talk with people about subjects she knew nothing about. However, she knew that God allowed information to come into her mind, translating those thoughts to words of comfort for hurting people. Whatever she spoke was what God wanted the person on the other end of the phone to hear. "All that I had to do was to be there and to be available," Dolores said.

When asked by Stephen Kiser if she could recall a specific conversation when someone called in, Dolores recalled that God had moved in many supernatural ways there at the TV station, and she watched with amazement when calls skipped over two phone stations just to get to the right person who could minister to that caller the best. She saw events like these happen innumerable times.

Chapter 4

MYSTICAL VISIONS

These views into other realms were transcribed from handwritten notes and e-mails sent to me by my aunt.

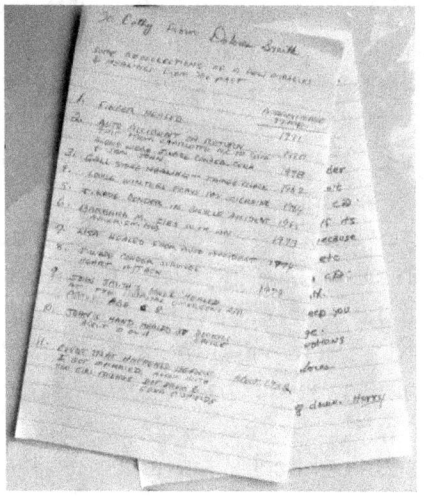

Looking on Washington, D.C.

While attending a weekly Christian meeting held in Cocoa, my Aunt Dolores recalled members of the group beginning to pray for the nation.

While those prayers were being sent up, Dolores had a vision. "Suddenly I was near the ceiling looking down onto the floor of the house where Congress meets.

"There were many men in fine looking suits, and I saw one fall out of his chair onto the floor and then on his face. While looking around the room, I saw men collapsing and falling to the floor one by one. Many got on their knees facing their chairs, but no one stayed seated.

"Some were in the aisles on their knees crying loudly, some were in front of their chairs on their knees sobbing, and a few were up at the front podium sobbing really loud. A few were trying to crawl away. There was so much noise in the large room that the sound of wailing and open crying was almost overwhelming. The glory of GOD was in the place, and guilt, plus revelation was taking place.

"I observed all this for a few minutes. There was not one man left seated, and each one was either lying prostrate on the floor or kneeling in front of their chairs. Then I heard, 'There will be no voting this day.'

"Suddenly, the scene changed to a large open area up in the sky where there was a huge table, which resembled stainless steel. This table was so long that it went miles into the distance.

"On this table were piles and piles of something, and I wondered what it was. There was an angel who held what looked like a small shovel in his hand and was busy raking up the piles and collecting them. Suddenly I knew that the piles were lots and lots of prayers sent to the throne room of God.

"They were all the prayers from Americans as appeals for this nation. Then this thought came to me,

'Will there be enough prayers to cause this scene in the Congress to take place?'

"The vision faded, and I was back in my seat and prayers were still going on in the room for our nation. At this time I had an understanding that the only way for a scene like this to take place was for the positive prayers of intercession to come forth.

"I also realized at the same time that some people were called to come against the darkness, but others were supposed to only intercede for the will of God to be done in this country. The vision impacted me so much that I could not speak for the better part of the meeting, or even share what I saw and heard until many days later."

When the Door Was Shut

A group of women gathered at the home of a friend and they all began to pray for one individual who was there.

"I was sitting at the back, praying in agreement with the group. Suddenly, I was observing another event. I saw the same lady who was being prayed for in a pitch-black basement that was very deep in the ground. I saw a very dim light begin to descend down a flight of stairs.

"Then Jesus became visible, and he was holding an old fashioned kerosene lantern with his finger in the holding ring. This was the dim light. I recall questioning why he was holding the lantern, when the light coming from the person of Jesus was brilliant and the lantern was pale in comparison.

"Then I saw there were a lot of doors all along the walls and they were all open. Jesus took his foot and one by one slammed each of the doors shut. Then he set down the lantern on the floor, went up the steps and only the dim light remained there.

"I did share this vision with the group, but no one knew what it meant."

Vision at a Funeral

"While attending a funeral service for an 18 year-old girl, I suddenly saw her in a huge open field with thousands of yellow flowers. She was running and leaping like a ballerina. I knew she was in heaven.

"The next day I went to the mother and related what I had seen. The mother told me that the girl had studied ballet for years and loved it, and that I was the third person who had told her they had seen this exact same vision! I did not know the girl, only the mother."

Fate of the Lost

"At a church service, a visiting evangelist was holding a series of meetings and this was the final meeting. I was sitting close to the front on the left side near the wall. When the appeal was made at the end of meeting for people to accept Christ as their Savior, the evangelist opened his arms wide as he spoke.

"Suddenly, I saw Jesus standing behind the man

with his arms opened. It was so awesome, that I could have viewed this forever. But suddenly, I wondered if anyone else saw this vision. It had already been a minute or two.

"I turned to look at the people, then the church turned jet black. Out of the blackness, there were only about four or five faces showing. All of a sudden, this meant that only those people of the 500 in attendance knew Jesus. Since this seemed impossible for me to accept, I had an enigma. I knew some of these people at the church, and surely that many could not be lost! It bothers me now, but God never told me anything to explain it."

Epilogue

On Miracles and Prayer

If the mysteries of God could be fully understood by men, it would be something bottled and made available on the shelves of our favorite store. We may never be able to fathom why God extends his favor to some and not others, or why some desperate prayers never get answered.

What we do know is what God's word says in the Bible, "His favor is for a lifetime or in His favor is life." (Psalm 30:5 AMP) Kingdoms have fallen out of God's favor throughout the ages by not giving thanks to God and keeping him first.

Jesus himself taught us a prayer, "Our Father which art in heaven, Hallowed be thy name. Thy kingdom come, Thy will be done in earth, as it is in heaven." Matthew 6:9-10. This tells us there is no sickness in heaven! So let us open the door of thanksgiving, while praying for the health of his people here on earth.
I believe there is someone praying for everyone on the planet, whether individually or collectively. God does hear the cries of desperate mothers, the helpless fathers, and the innocent prayers of kids lifting up "all the children of the world." There may be extreme pain, suffering and loss but how much worse would it be without prayers calling for miracles?

Now all glory to God, who is able, through his mighty power at work within us, to accomplish infinitely more than we might ask or think.
I Peter 3:20 NLT

Nuggets from Dolores

We must remember that to God, there are no miracles, just His hand intervening in a second of time.

What is awesome is that God pays attention to us in our daily walk and when we are about His business, He is especially interested.

If we are one of His, we get angelic help in ordinary circumstances.

There are many Christians I know who have had similar experiences, and we are all ordinary, everyday people.

Dolores' Favorite Bible verses

And we know that all things work together for good to them that love God, to them that are called according to His purposes.
Romans 8:28

For I am persuaded, that neither death, nor life, nor angels, nor principalities, nor powers, nor things present, nor things to come, nor height nor depth, nor any other creature, shall be able to separate us from the love of God, which is in Christ Jesus our Lord.
Romans 8:38-39

For God so loved the world that He gave His only begotten son, that whosoever believeth in Him should not perish, but have everlasting life.
John 3:16

But seek ye first the kingdom of God, and His righteousness, and all these things shall be added unto you.
Matthew 6:33

About the Author

Cathy Rodgers lives on a tidal creek in Savannah, Georgia where she experiences the daily ebb and flow of life on the saltwater marsh. She enjoys writing, photography, gardening and creating websites and blogs in her company called Seven Waves Marketing.

She is passionate about her faith and helping others with their health and weight loss challenges through a blog called Cathy Chats.

She refers to herself as, "Just a praying grandmother passing these miracles on to the next generation."

"One generation will praise your deeds to another..." Psalm 145:4.

You can find Cathy at www.CathyChats.com

Our Written Lives
book publishing services
www.owlofhope.com

www.ingramcontent.com/pod-product-compliance
Lightning Source LLC
Chambersburg PA
CBHW071224070526
44584CB00019B/3141